10.

9.

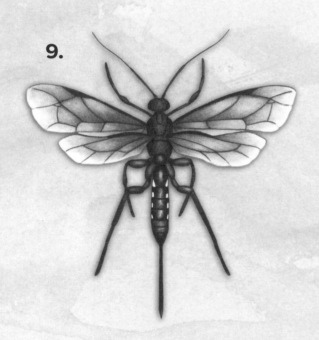

11.

7. Sand wasp

8. Potter wasp

9. Orchid dupe wasp

10. Cuckoo wasp

11. Cicada-killer wasp

For every child who loves bugs. Keep caring. – KG

For Mum and Dad, who have cheered me on
right from the start. – SH

A catalogue record for this book is available from the National Library of Australia.

ISBN: 9781486315734 (hbk)
ISBN: 9781486315741 (epdf)
ISBN: 9781486315758 (epub)

Published by:
CSIRO Publishing
Private Bag 10
Clayton South VIC 3169
Australia

Telephone: +61 3 9545 8400
Email: publishing.sales@csiro.au
Website: www.publish.csiro.au
Sign up to our email alerts: publish.csiro.au/earlyalert

Edited by Dr Kath Kovac
Cover, text design and layout by Cath Pirret Design
Printed in China by Leo Paper Products Ltd

The views expressed in this publication are those of the author and illustrator and do not necessarily represent those of, and should not be attributed to, the publisher or CSIRO.

CSIRO acknowledges the Traditional Owners of the lands that we live and work on across Australia and pays its respect to Elders past and present. CSIRO recognises that Aboriginal and Torres Strait Islander peoples have made and will continue to make extraordinary contributions to all aspects of Australian life including culture, economy and science. CSIRO is committed to reconciliation and demonstrating respect for Indigenous knowledge and science. The use of Western science in this publication should not be interpreted as diminishing the knowledge of plants, animals and environment from Indigenous ecological knowledge systems.

Author's acknowledgements
Thank you to Steve Crawford and Adrian Sherriff of the Aussie Wildlife Show Podcast for caring about the planet and its creatures, big and small. Thank you to fellow author Dr Anne Morgan for her encouragement. Lastly, enormous thanks to Dr Erinn Fagan-Jeffries for her inspiration, expertise and infectious enthusiasm.

Note for readers: Scientific terms are explained in the glossary at the end of the book.

Note for teachers: Teacher notes are available at: https://www.publish.csiro.au/book/8057/#forteachers

WONDERFUL WASPS

KATRINA GERMEIN

Illustrated by
SUZANNE HOUGHTON

CSIRO
PUBLISHING

What do you know about wasps?

Not the plain, European 'we're-everywhere' wasps,
but the 'we-have-always-been-here' wasps.

The colourful, wonderful,
weird Aussie wasps!

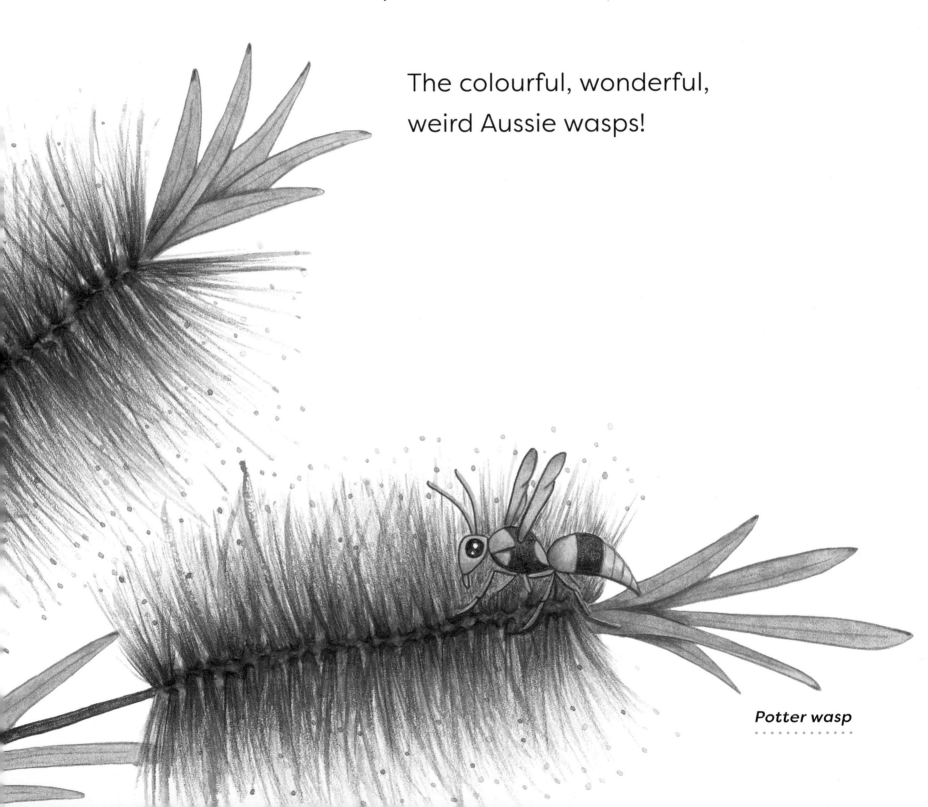

Potter wasp

You most likely know little.
There's little that's known.
They're so hard to study.
They're tiny when grown.

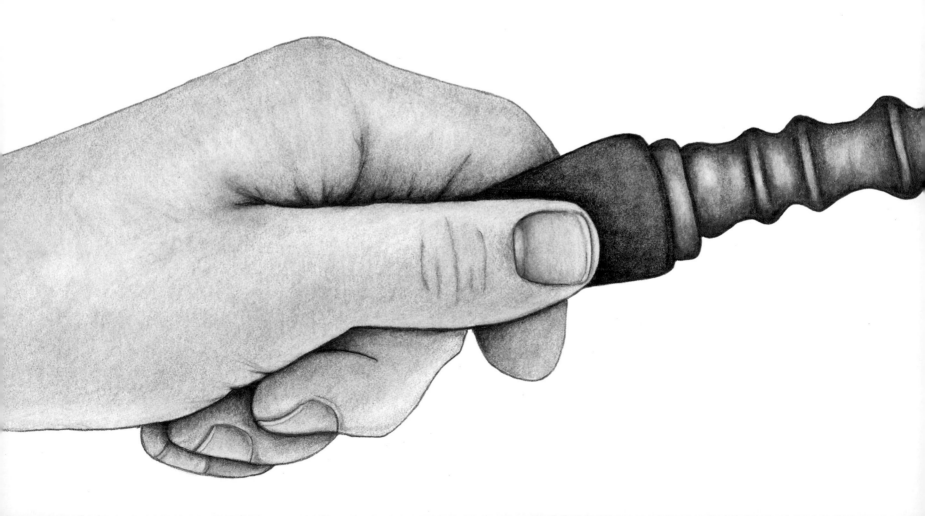

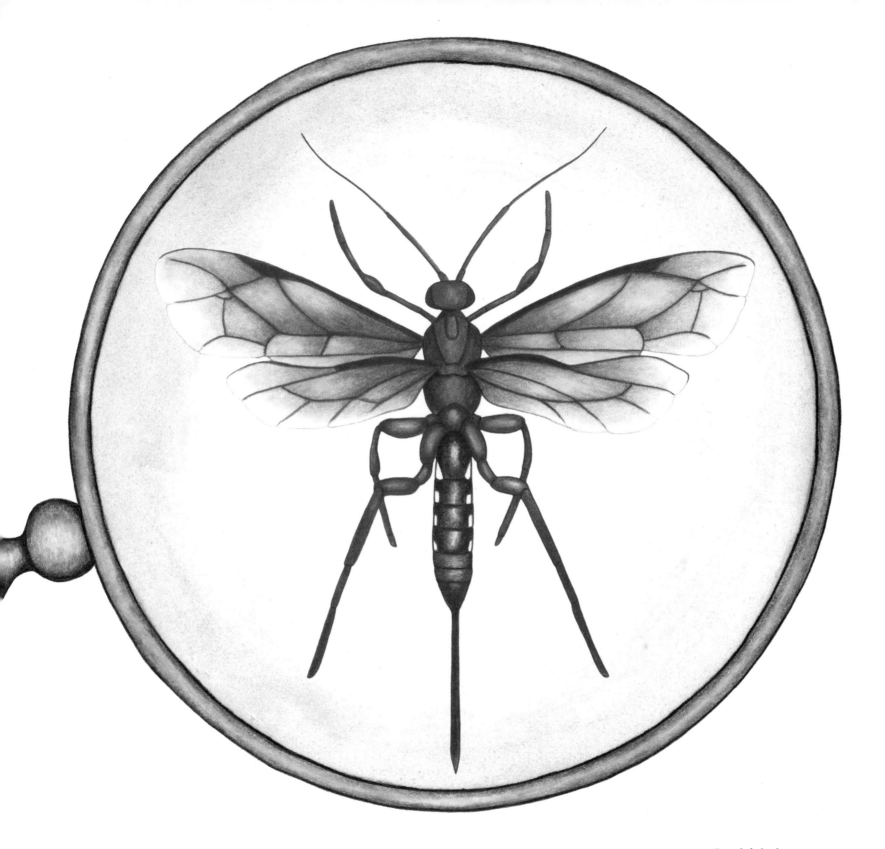

Orchid dupe wasp

Orchid dupe wasp

Fig wasp

Paper wasp

There are hundreds, no thousands,
of native wasps here.
Can you tell me about them?
Any ideas?

Potter wasp

Orange spider wasp

Cicada-killer wasp

Mud-dauber wasp

Blue flower wasp

Cuckoo wasp

But why does it matter?
What do they do?

They're not furry and strong

like a wombat

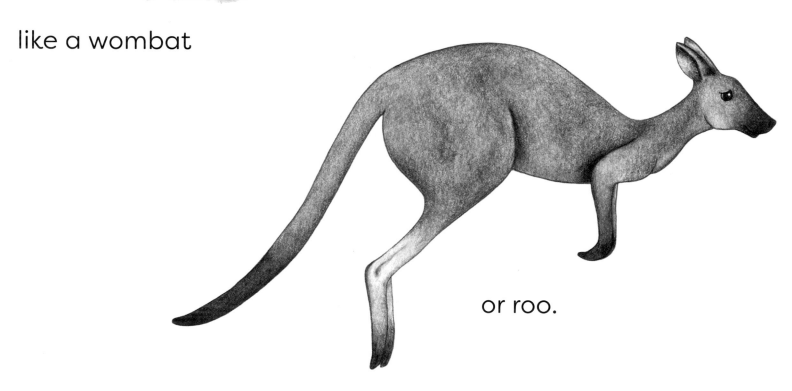

or roo.

They're not cute like koalas,
or seen as inspiring ...

Wasps are just wasps,
yet their work
is quite tiring.

Sand wasp

They're sky pollinators,
like fruit bats and bees,
helping our planet so plants can make seeds.

Lots of the flora that's living today
would simply stop growing if wasps
went away.

And think of the fauna that feed on the shrubs,
or live in the trees, like gliders and grubs.

If wasps disappear,
the plants could go too.

Then what are those animals
going to do?

Some other critters love to eat wasps.
Without little insects, their dinner is lost.

When lizards

and birds

and dragonflies dine –
a juicy-fresh wasp
can suit them just fine.

Orange spider wasp

Spiders are food that many wasps need.
They paralyse spiders so larvae can feed.

A wasp lays an egg right onto a spider.
The baby wasp hatches and feeds from outside her!
(Think that sounds gross? It's what parasites do,
and they need to eat, like me and like you.)

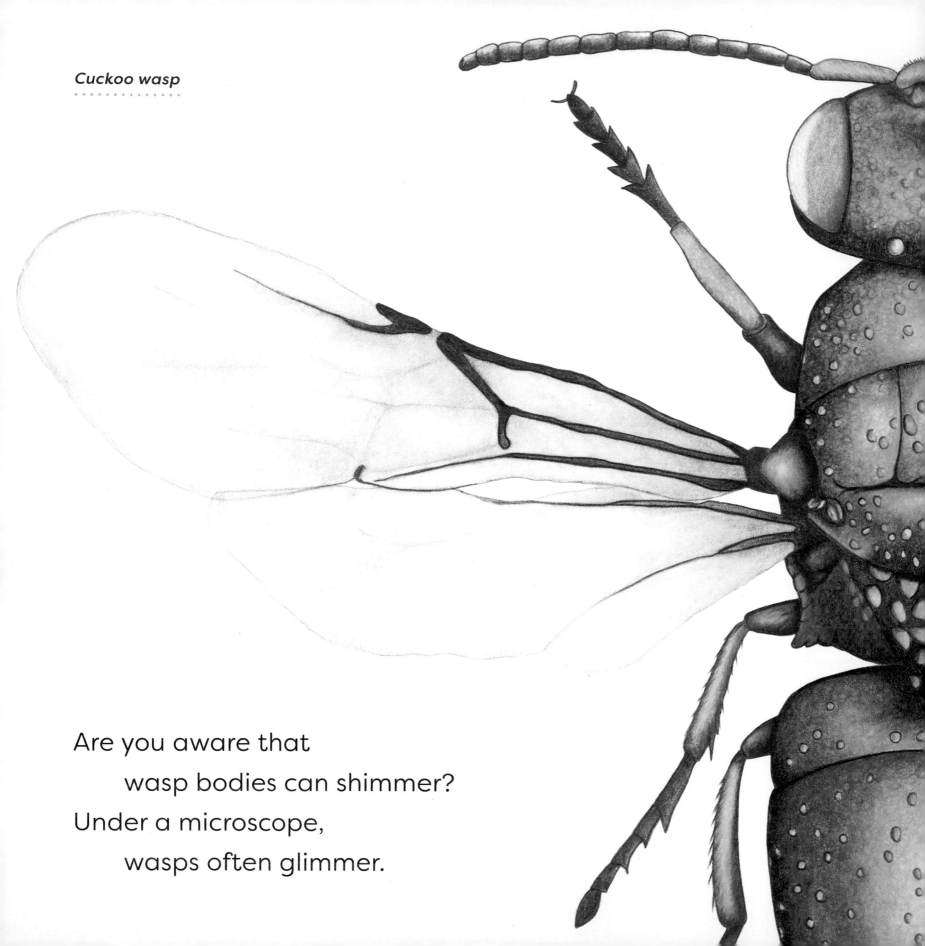

Cuckoo wasp

Are you aware that
　　wasp bodies can shimmer?
Under a microscope,
　　wasps often glimmer.

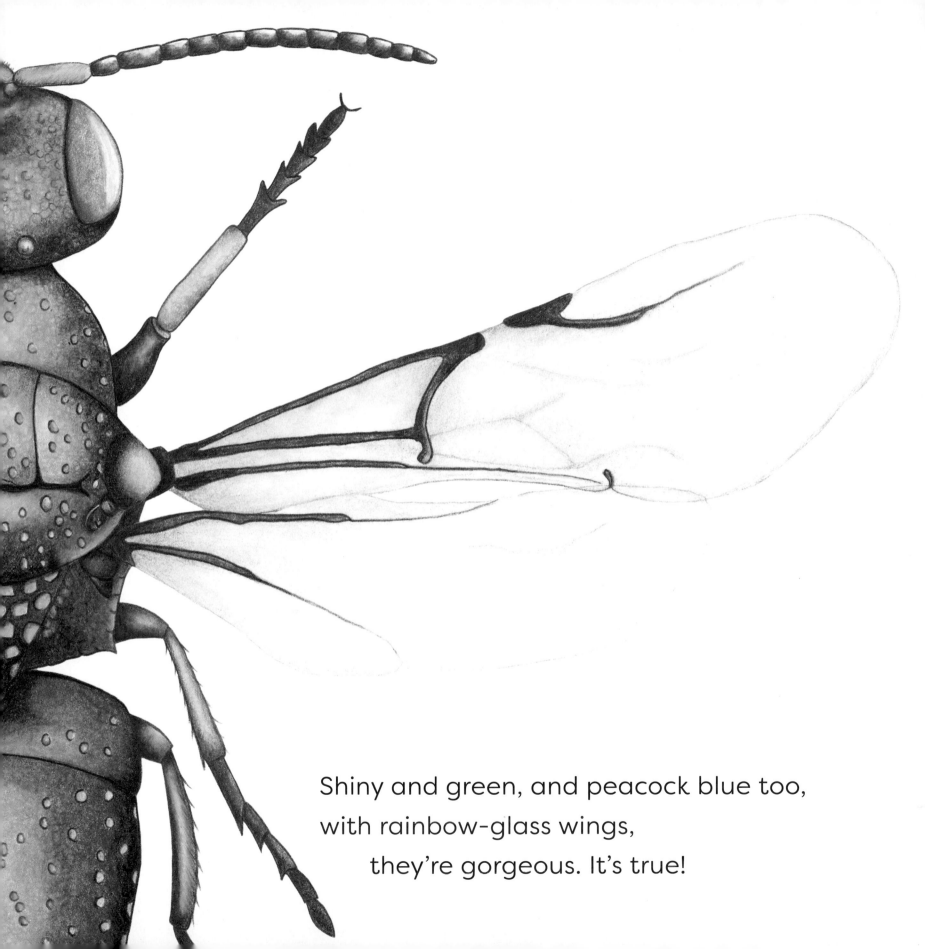

Shiny and green, and peacock blue too,
with rainbow-glass wings,
       they're gorgeous. It's true!

It's best not to touch them (some wasps like to sting).
Leave them alone and they'll just do their thing.

You may be allergic, so keep a big space
for you and the wasp – don't get in its face.

Blue flower wasp

Each tiny wasp needs a safe home.

When you spy mud cocoons,
please leave them alone.

Those hexagonal nests
are paper wasp ranches ...

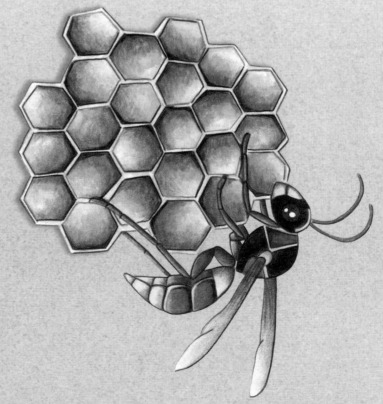

... and native fig wasps need fruit on fig branches.

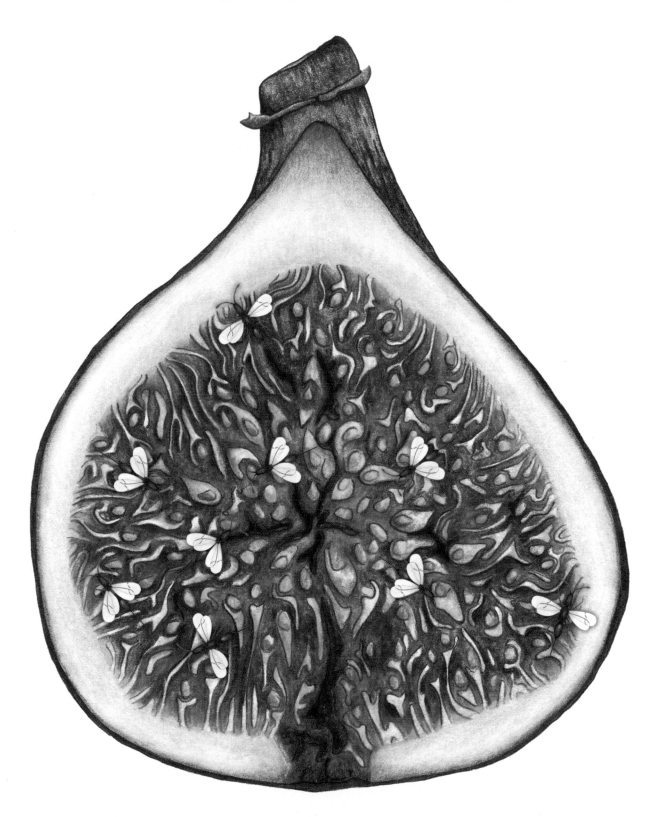

Like beetles and ants and butterflies do,
wasps need healthy bushland
to live and grow, too.

Why not plant a garden with natives that bloom?
And give Aussie wasps just a little more room.

So ... What do you know about wasps?

MORE ABOUT AUSTRALIAN WASPS

Wasps are insects found all around the world. They live across Australia in bushland, cities, parks and gardens, and even in your own backyard or school.

Australia has more than 12 000 species of native wasps. They are members of an order of insects called Hymenoptera, which also includes sawflies, bees and ants. The insects in this order have strong mouthparts, called mandibles, to chew or cut their food, and usually have four thin, translucent wings.

Wasps are generally small to medium-sized, although some are almost too tiny to see, such as diapriid wasps, which resemble small, flying ants. Larger wasps, like the cicada-killer wasp, can grow up to 4 centimetres long. That's as long as a match!

Although a wasp's life cycle varies between species, it has four main stages, like other Hymenoptera. All wasps begin as an egg. The wasp that hatches from the egg is called the larva, or grub. Over time the larva pupates, which means it changes into another form called a pupa. Finally it transforms into an adult wasp, ready to emerge from the nest.

Wasps and the environment

Wasps play an important role in helping to control insect and spider populations. For example, many wasps are parasites, laying their eggs inside paralysed insects, including spiders. The wasp larvae grow up feeding on the live insects. If we didn't have wasps, we'd have many, many more insects!

Most adult wasps feed on nectar – the sugary liquid found in flowers. Some pollen from the flowers sticks to the wasps as they feed, and they spread it between plants as they move around. This is how wasps pollinate flowers and help new seeds to grow.

Another reason wasps are so important to the environment is that they are a food source for countless other animals.

Aussie wasps need us to protect their habitat so they have somewhere to live. If you make space in your garden for Australian plants, you will also be supporting other native wildlife, such as lizards and birds. Most native plants need less water than introduced plants, so by helping wasps and other creatures you will also be conserving water.

How do we know about wasps?

Scientists who study wasps are called entomologists. They also study other insects and spiders, and describe and name new species when they are discovered. Entomologists look at the role of insects such as wasps in different environments and ecosystems, and study how they interact with other animals and plants.

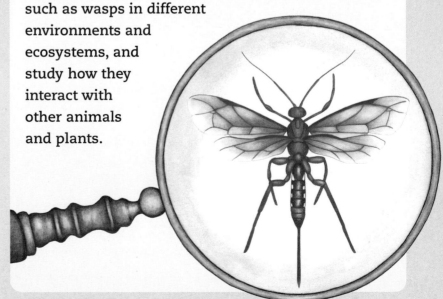

Some of the wasps in this story

Spider wasps (Family Pompilidae)

Female spider wasps capture spiders for their babies to eat. The mother moves quickly, walking or hopping, until she finds a spider to sting and paralyse. She drags the paralysed spider to a nest, usually a small hollow. She then lays an egg in the spider's abdomen and closes up the nest with mud or dirt. When the wasp larva hatches, it feeds on the spider's insides.

Australia has many spider wasp species, which pollinate native plants and control spider populations. They are not aggressive towards humans and rarely sting people.

Native paper wasps (Family Vespidae)

Paper wasps live in colonies, and often build nests in carports, sheds and around houses. People commonly destroy these nests. However, if left alone, paper wasps will not harm you. Instead, they will help you control pests in your garden – finding aphids, flies and other bugs for their larvae to eat.

Mud-dauber wasps (*Sceliphron laetum*)

Mud-dauber wasps are found all over Australia. They create nests using a combination of saliva and mud or clay. Rows of mud cells are built into the nest, and then each cell is filled with a paralysed invertebrate, such as a spider or caterpillar. These are for the wasp larvae to feed on when they hatch from the egg.

Cuckoo wasps (Family Chrysididae)

Many different species of cuckoo wasps are found across Australia. *Stilbum cyanurum* is the largest, and some would say the prettiest. Cuckoo wasps are bright green, blue or purple, often appearing iridescent. They are sometimes referred to by the nickname of emerald wasp. The females lay their eggs in the nest of another insect – including other wasps, such as the mud-dauber wasp. When baby cuckoo wasps hatch, they eat the host larvae, or food that is stored in the nest for the host larvae.

Native fig wasps (Family Agaonidae)

Without native fig wasps there would be no native fig trees, because fig trees rely on wasps for pollination. The fig wasp also needs the fig trees to complete their life cycle. The male and female fig wasp mate inside a fig, which has tiny flowers inside. The female then flies away to lay her egg within another fig, pollinating the flowers with pollen she picked up from the first fig. When the larva hatches inside the fig, it feeds on the fruit as it grows!

European wasps (*Vespula germanica*)

The introduced European wasps are considered dangerous pests. Aggressive and with a painful sting, they are attracted to human picnic fare, such as meat, sweet food and drink.

Many people confuse European and native wasps, but Australian wasps rarely hurt people, and some can't even sting. However, some native wasps will inflict a painful sting if provoked, and can sting more than once!

European wasps live in large, communal nests, unlike most Australian wasps, who are usually solitary creatures – except for paper wasps and mud-dauber wasps. If you're not sure about what kind of wasp or nest you've discovered, keep a distance to be safe. If you tamper with a European wasp nest, they will attack you, so always contact a professional pest company to help.

GLOSSARY

Bushland: A large area of land where mainly native plants grow, providing habitat for native animals.

Cocoon: A silky case that an insect larva creates to protect itself while it transforms into an adult.

Ecosystem: An interconnected group of living things that interact with the environment and each other in a given area.

Fauna: All of the animals living in a particular area.

Flora: All of the plants growing in a particular area.

Gliders: Possum-like animals that are active at night. They live in trees and glide between branches.

Grub: A newly hatched insect that looks like a fat worm.

Habitat: The place where a plant or animal lives with all the things it needs, including water, food and shelter.

Insect: A small animal with three body parts, jointed legs and an external skeleton.

Invertebrate: An animal without a backbone.

Iridescent: Showing colours on surfaces which appear to change when viewed from different angles, like you see on a soap bubble.

Larva (plural larvae): A young insect that has left the egg, yet still looks very different from the mature insect.

Life cycle: The series of developmental changes that a living thing experiences throughout its life.

Microscope: An instrument that enlarges an image of an object so that small details can be seen.

Native plant/animal: A plant or animal that has existed naturally in an area for thousands of years.

Nest: A shelter animals make for their eggs, and sometimes a place where they live as well.

Paralyse: To make part of an animal's body, or its whole body, unable to move while it is still alive.

Parasite: A living thing that lives on or in another living thing and feeds from that host, often harming it.

Pollinator: An animal that moves pollen between male and female flower parts.

Species: A group of living things that have similar characteristics and can breed with each other to produce young that can also successfully breed.

Sting: Pain caused by a plant or animal when it pierces or brushes a person's skin, sometimes with poison.

1. Blue flower wasp
2. Paper wasp
3. Orange spider wasp
4. Mud-dauber wasp
5. European wasp
6. Fig wasp